Outside My Comfort Zone

LINDSAY WAXMAN

Copyright © 2024 Lindsay Waxman
All rights reserved
First Edition

Fulton Books
Meadville, PA

Published by Fulton Books 2024

ISBN 979-8-89427-347-1 (paperback)
ISBN 979-8-89427-348-8 (digital)

Printed in the United States of America

To my mother Mindy:
Through all my mistakes and health issues,
you stood by me and never wavered.
Grateful for your love and you!

To Brittany:
Thank you for showing me what it means
to be such a strong human being. That
no matter how hard situations get, you
should never give up on life or yourself!

To my aunt Lisa:
You are one of the main reasons why I'm not
afraid to tell people my story about my health
background, and I saw how much you fought to
have the best life for yourself! Thank you for being
one of the most significant influences in my life.

To my great-grandmother Ruth:
Thank you for helping me keep your memory alive every single day and showing me what it truly means to be such a giving and loving individual. I miss you every day.

To Angela:
I know I wasn't your first choice for a camper, but I'm truly glad the Fates brought us together. You are the most down-to-earth person I know. I have so much love and respect for you! I love you, Chug Along. Thanks for letting me be your Cubby!

Contents

Chapter 1 1

> I used to hate fitting in until I realized
> I was born to stand out.
> —Matt Haig

Chapter 2 31

> You might not win every battle. There are going
> to be some really tough days. There might be
> several tough times in any given single day, but
> hopefully, this will help somebody think, *This isn't
> easy; it is a fight, but I'm going to keep fighting it.*
> —Jared Padalecki

Chapter 3 61

> Life is like a camera. Focus on what's
> important and you will capture it perfectly.
> —Josh Hutcherson

I used to hate fitting in until I realized
I was born to stand out.
—Matt Haig

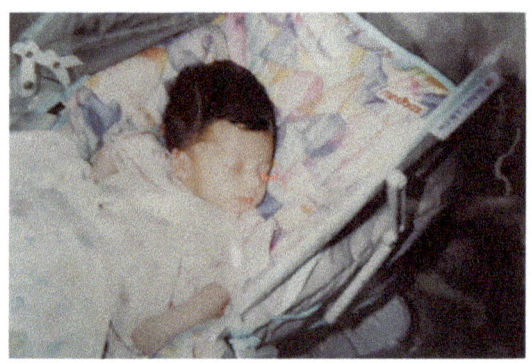

In the quiet at 2:30 in the morning, Superman flying on the TV screen
My mother bravely brought me into this world, unseen
No doctors or nurses, just her strength and love
Bringing me forth with a power from above
With just one push, she held onto hope
Knowing that soon, I would be able to cope Superman flying high, saving the day
As my mother brought me into the world in her own special way.
In just twenty minutes, a miracle occurred
My father cutting through my mom's umbilical cord
With tears in my mother's eyes, she held me tight
Grateful for the gift of new life, shining bright.

Three hours later ending up at the grocery store
The cashier asking my mother, "Am I losing it, or weren't you pregnant before?"
My mother replied, "I just had the baby today, I just needed to go shopping,"
Hysterically giggling without stopping.
From there, it was all hugs, kisses, and cuddles from what I truly believed to be the most incredible journey
Not realizing how many obstacles it would take me to finally know if my life was worthy.

This was just the beginning…
In a world of whispers and shifting light
I wandered, feeling out of place, out of sight.
Mismatched puzzle pieces, a mind apart,
Struggling to connect, longing for a better start.
Through swirling thoughts and silent screams,
I navigated in and out of a labyrinth of dreams.
Patterns emerged in a kaleidoscope hue,
Revealing a truth I never knew.
In a room of gentle light, the news was told,
A doctor's soft voice, tender and bold.
To an eleven-year-old girl, "You're fine, you have autism."
Not realizing, how do I figure out my own type of rhythm?

Confusion dancing in my dark brown eyes,
Questioning all the what-ifs and whys.
The doctor smiled, her heart sincere,
Guiding me through my own shadows of fear.
Telling me to "embrace my colors, let them shine.
In every hue, try to find your own sunshine.

Autism is a different type of view.
Your journey waits, pure and true."
With each revelation, a new path unfurled,
Embracing the colors that defined my new perspective in my world.
Acceptance bloomed in a slow and gentle bloom,
Empowering me to break free from what I thought was my own doom.

To them:
"You don't look autistic?"
"Wow, you must be really high functioning!"
"My friend has kids with autism, and you don't behave anything like them."

Me:
Thanks!
The years of bullying and abuse really paid off.
I finally learned to never display my vulnerabilities.
I learned that others would be ashamed or uncomfortable of my differences,
Try to take advantage of my disability.
I suppose I should thank all those who thought it would be perfectly satisfying to hurt me.

I now internalize, minimize, and conceal every difficulty.
I have been taught to sacrifice my own health and well-being
For the sake of others' needs to remain oblivious and prejudiced.
Thank you for reminding me that
All that hard work and pain were worth it for you

Who can operate in this public space
Unburdened by my challenges
Oblivious to my suffering?
As a child,
My skills were less finely honed.
I had not yet developed the craft of invisibility.
One might have guessed me autistic,
But the assumption was more often
Some combination of naughty and lazy.
Don't pretend to have sympathy for those with autism
When a comment clearly shows
It wasn't there.
Let's be clear too.
High functioning means highly camouflaged
Easily forgotten
Lost under the cruelty of others.
It does not mean low difficulty.

On the road from North to South Florida
A journey filled with sun and flora
From loads of land to extremely scorch
I didn't realize that my head was about to go off like a blowtorch.
Going to see friends from years ago
Feeling like my head was about ready to blow
Not knowing that my seizures would come upon fast
Scared for this event to be truly vast.
Falling off my chair, my body shook, mind in haze,
I prayed for the seizures to end this craze
My mother catching me and saving my head
Covering my face from other people's view, not wanting this to be a front-page news spread.
My mother got me in the car and drove me home

Not realizing this was the beginning of what I thought
    would be the true definition of the death zone
Calling my dad, my mom caught my arms from the
    front
Dad from the back
My seizures were continuing their unholy attack

My brain would not stop seizing
Wishing that my seizures would be easing.
Mom driving me all the way from Ocala to Miami
Feeling like this day was a call from winning my first
    Grammy.

Having seizures is an extreme stride
But remembering them was entirely the longest ride
Flashing back, recalling just being in my mom's car
Laying down in the smoky colored seat way too far.
Closing my eyes, trying to tell my brain to quit the episodes

Trying to give myself the permission to please stop,
   to feel abode.
It was like I was fighting my own self to stay robust
Wishing, praying to the tiniest electron in my brain,
   "I don't want to be six feet under in dust."
Hastening through traffic, swerving around cars
Keeping calm while distinctly driving afar
Checking every few minutes to make sure I'm secure
My mother keeps her emotions obscure.
Blacking out and coming back
Reminiscing a state trooper with the perfect mustache shades of black

Pulling me out to put me in a big red-and-white chopper
Knowing how to handle me with the procedures that they performed perfectly proper.
I don't remember all of it
   But the parts I continuously reminisce, I pushed myself to never quit
   Mom explained to me all of what persisted to occur
   But I would have imagined a lot of this event would seem like a questioning blur.

Just like the stars at night
Just like the vast ocean
Just like the strands of your hair
My love for you
Is never-ending.
Just like the rain that drips
Just like the sand that flows with the wind, just like
    the numbers that we count
My love for you
Is never-ending.
Just like the clouds at daytime
Just like the rays of the sun
Just like the people around us
My love for you

Is never-ending.
How can you stop
My love that is never-ending?
Oh, I know now
It's because you don't feel
The same way I do.
You never did.
And thanks to you, I love myself more.

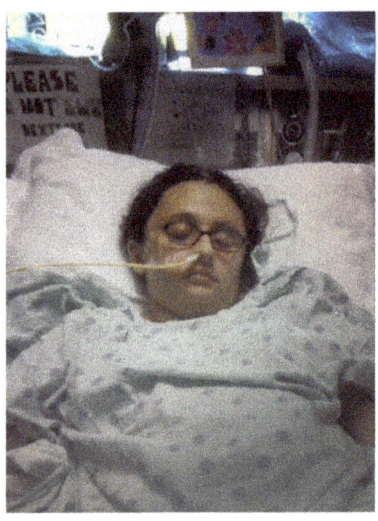

Over two hundred seizures later, the doctor thinking
    it's time to shut off my brain
Giving me rest to feel a lot less astrain
Tubes and wires from my brain and arms to the machine
Helping me breathe to keep my body a lot more
    serene
Not understanding what's going on outside my mind
In a labyrinth hoping to find.
Going through, pushing through thick barricades
Praying to break through the mistakes I made in
    these past two decades
I walked through different doors of my youth

Panicking, trying to find someone to help me find my own truth
I finally find a pure and soothing light
Not knowing would bring me closer to happiness in sight.
Out of the blissful and luminescent gleam
Truly feeling like I was having one of the greatest dreams

It was my great-grandmother
A reuniting hug, we squeeze and embrace each other
She tells me, "I've missed you with all my heart
I never want to spend another minute apart
If you see the light, that means you're ready
I think we spent enough time apart already."
My grandmother puts out her hand with calming bliss
Putting my hand out, not realizing what I was about to miss
I look down, watching my mom talking to me in my slumber
Wishing that my surgery was not her biggest blunder.
I look back up at my grandmother with painful regret
Telling her, "I'm sorry, I just can't leave Mom yet…"
With the hardest decision and a teary goodbye
I held her tight promising I wouldn't cry.
She goes back into the light with final goodbyes
And I get pulled back and I open my eyes.

I am someone who gives all she has every time.
I am someone who talks twice as much as she listens.
I am someone who will tell you what you mean to her on a dime.
I am someone who is nice and caring, whose shadow glistens.
I am someone who can expect nothing and give you everything.
I am someone who knows what she wants.
I am someone who has dreams like Martin Luther King.
I am someone who is as warm as a basket of croissants.

I am someone who wears her heart on her sleeve. I am someone who gets taken advantage of.

I am someone who has never had a kiss on New Year's Eve.

I am someone who is ready to fall in love.

I am someone who believes in honesty and trust. I am someone who loves everything she does.

I am someone who believes that self-happiness and love are a must.

I am someone who tries to be fair and just.

I am someone who is ready to take on anything.

I am someone who is telling you who I am.

I am someone who has that crazy little extra zing. I am someone who can be your grand slam.

You can watch me stay or watch me go, but this is who I am.

In the depths of my soul, I search for the truth
To uncover the layers of my youth
It's like continuously giving money to a tollbooth
To peel back the masks that I wear
And confront the shadows lurking there
To truly know that all that happened, I am dolefully aware
Through the tangled maze of my mind
I navigate, hoping to find
The key to unlocking all my hidden fears
And face them head-on, despite all the past mistakes that appear.
In the mirror, I see a reflection

Of a person on the blink of introspection
I confront my flaws, my insecurities
And embrace the journey of self-discovery
And apologize to those for blaming them for my not-so-full recovery.
I welcome the challenges that come my way
For they are the stepping stones that lead to my growth each day

I rise above the doubts and the pain
And emerge stronger, with a newfound reign.
Through the trials and tribulations that I face
I learn to lean into the discomfort, to embrace
The unknown, the unfamiliar, the uncharted
And emerge transformed, ready to be open-hearted.
So here's to the journey of self-discovery
To grow, to face challenges with bravery.
May we continue to evolve and thrive
As we uncover the truths that make us feel alive.
I may not be able to see what others see
But I want…
No not want,
I need to remember who I chose to be.
I want to be the pure bliss of my favorite song.
The tear that falls down with happiness looking at a painting that no artist could paint wrong.

To be the reason even if someone is having a bad day
One smile and all the hardships go away.
I am not my mistakes, but I will make them
Not in anger, simply in the best way.
To laugh at them and brush them away.

You are not your name
Or height or how much you weigh
Or even gender.
You are not an age
And you are not where you are from.
You are your favorite books
And the songs that get stuck in your head.
You are your thoughts

And what you enjoy eating for breakfast
On Saturday mornings.
You are thousands of things
But everyone chooses
To see the million things
You are *not*.

Life is like an old house; it gets used,
Worn-out and old.
Then it's time to move to another.
Life is just a place where your soul lives
While it's on Earth.
When your soul gets tired of living on Earth,
It finds a new home.
As time goes by, so does your life.
So live life to the fullest, and don't let a day go by
Without cherishing every moment.

Perfection was created
To make us feel imperfect
But imperfect, of course,
Is the perfect thing to be.
We spend every hour of every day,
Every day of every week,
Trying to be different,
Trying to "feel" unique.
Our nature is to search
For answers to life's questions.
Concepts we don't quite understand
Like "What is perfection?"
You strive to be "perfect,"
A term you honestly don't understand yet.
You should be yourself,
Don't let it be too late.

Surely happiness is a priority,
Over a word like "perfection."
So ask yourself this,
Who looks back at your reflection?

Life is pure insanity
And extremely unpredictable…
It's going to consistently push you over
Kick you while you're down
And hit you when you're endlessly trying to get back up.
Not everything can beat you
God is going to try and test you
But you get to choose which ones you let change you.
Listen to your heart

Follow your dreams
And let no one tell you what you're capable of. Push the limits
Break the rules
And enjoy every damn minute of it!
Laugh at everything
Live for as long as you can. Love all
But trust none.
Believe in yourself
And never lose faith in others

Settle for nothing but the best
And give 110% in everything you do.
Take risks
Live on the edge,
Yet stay safe
And cherish every freaking moment of it!
Life is a gift
Appreciate all the rewards
And jump on every opportunity.
Challenge everything
And fight for what you believe.
Back down for no one and nothing
But give in to the little things in life.
After all, that is what makes you… you.
Forget the unnecessary

But remember everything
Bring it with you everywhere you go.
Learn something new every day
And appreciate criticism.
Hate nothing and no one
But dislike what you want.

Never forget where you come from
And always remember where you are going.
Live life to the fullest
And have a reason for everything
Even if it's completely insane.
Find your purpose in life,
And *go for it*!

You might not win every battle. There are going to be some really tough days. There might be several tough times in any given single day, but hopefully, this will help somebody to think, *This isn't easy; it is a fight, but I'm going to keep fighting it.*
—Jared Padalecki

Never trust a mirror
For a mirror always lies
It makes you think that that all you're worth
Can be only seen from the outside.
Never trust a mirror
It only shows you what's skin-deep
You can't see how your eyelids flutter drifting off to sleep.
It doesn't show you what the world sees
When you're only being you
Or how your eyes light up
When you are loving what you do.
It doesn't capture the essence of when you're smiling
Where no one else can see

And your reflection cannot tell you
Everything you meant to me.
Never trust a mirror
For it only shows the skin
And if you think that it dictates your worth
It's time you look within.

I embarked on a journey, body and soul.
Through hardcore therapy, I pushed on,
To reclaim my strength, my spirit shone.
Physical therapy, a grueling test,
But I persevered, gave it my best.
Relearning to walk, to move with grace,
Each step a triumph,
In this challenging race.
Occupational therapy, hands at work,
Rebuilding skills with diligence and perks.
Tasks once simple, now a mountain to climb,
But I climbed with courage, one step at a time.

Speech therapy, a battle of words,
Struggling to communicate, my voice was unheard.
But with patience and practice, I found my way,
Speaking with confidence, each and every day.

Through the pain and the tears, I fought on,
Determined to heal, to rise like the dawn.
With each session, I grew stronger and free,
Embracing the journey, the new me.
So here I stand, a survivor, a fighter,
Through therapy's fire, I emerged brighter.
Epilepsy may have tried to bring me down,
But through therapy's strength, I wear victory's crown.

36 | Lindsay Waxman

Outside My Comfort Zone | 37

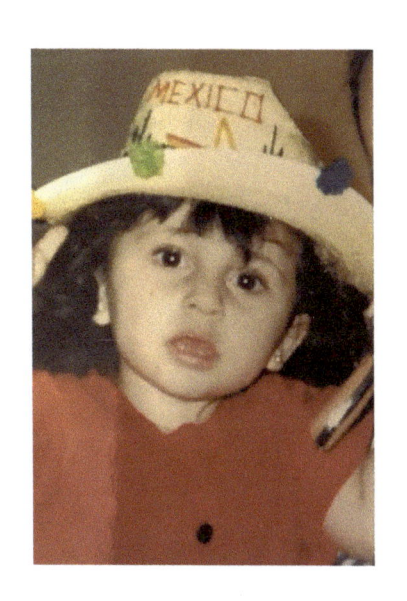

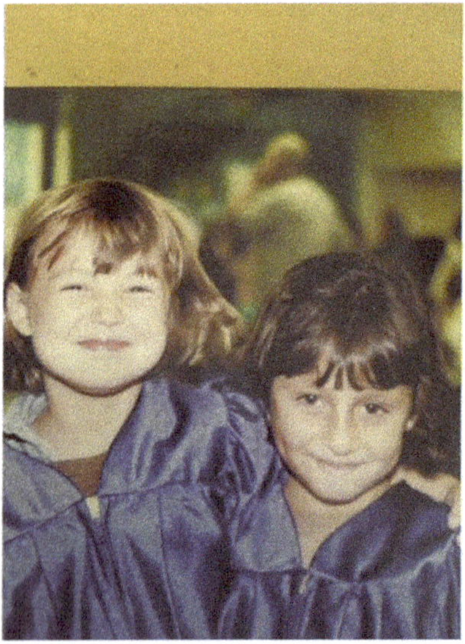

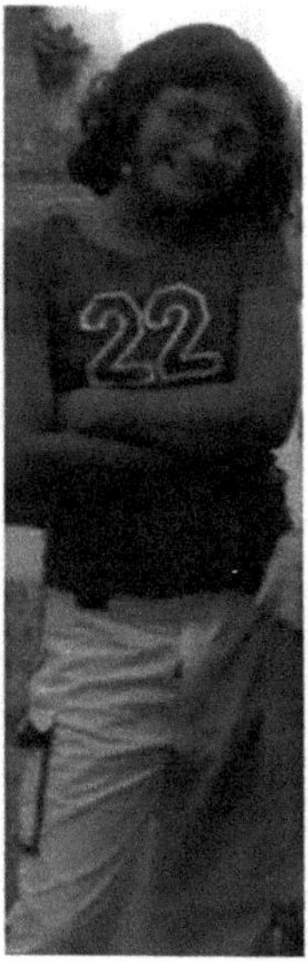

22

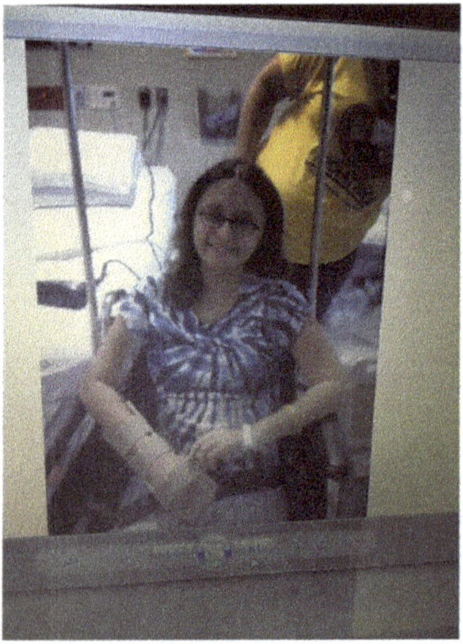

Outside My Comfort Zone | 41

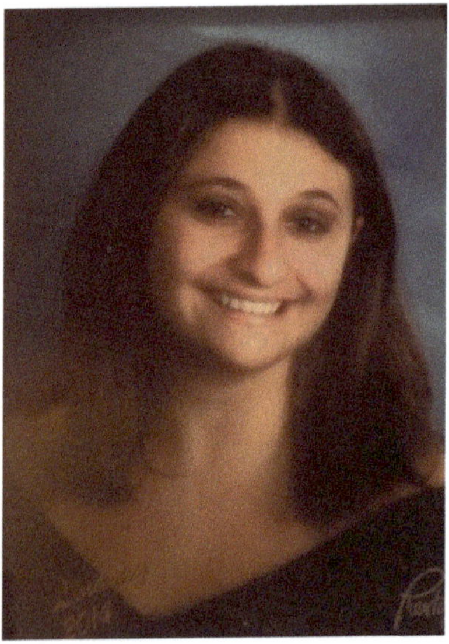

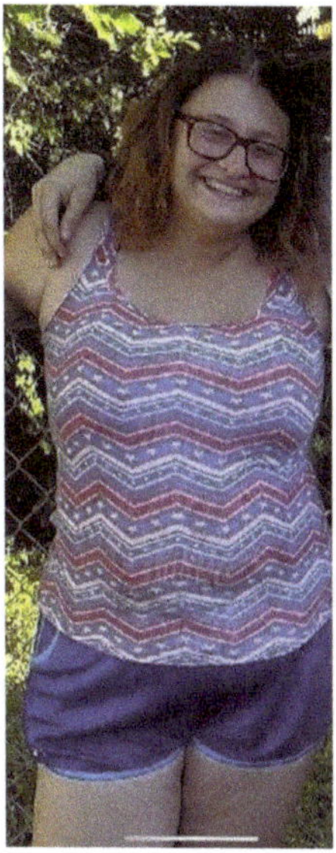

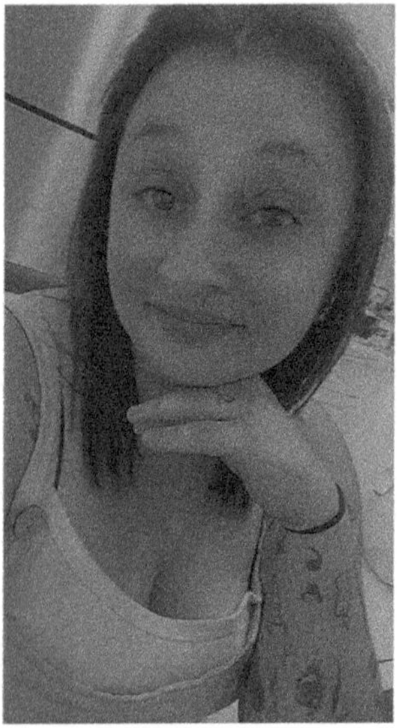

In a classroom, where we first met
Her eyes ablaze with a fiery threat
I had spoken to her boyfriend, you see
And with extreme rage, she was not pleased with me.
She brandished a knife, sharp and cold
Threatening to cut me, so bold
But two weeks later, to my surprise
We became the best of allies.
Our bond grew strong, our friendship true
From rocky start, something new
She apologized for her initial attack
And after that, we never looked back.

Through thick and thin, we stood side by side
Laughing, crying, with nothing to hide
What started as threat turned into love
My best friend sent from above.
So don't judge a book by its cover, they say
For sometimes the best friendships come from a fray
And though our beginning was rough and wild
I wouldn't trade it for anything, my crazy dear friend and I.
Fifteen years later, we are still going strong.
We can't push each other away, so what could truly go wrong?

I trusted you, I thought you were my friend
But you introduced me to what I didn't know would be my darkest end
A guy who was seven years older, whom I hardly knew,
Not realizing you took away my sense of safety, the plan you "drew."
Just weeks after my surgery, I was vulnerable and weak
You brought him to me, you didn't speak
Of the torturous endangerment that lurked in his eyes

Of the pure evil that hid behind his lies.
He snatched what wasn't his, he left me broken
He threatened to kill my family and friends, and he
    left me unspoken
I thought I could trust you, thinking you cared
But you betrayed me and left me scared.

I can never forgive the pain that you caused
The scars you left, the innocence lost
But I rose above and found my strength
To heal this wound in every length.
I reclaimed back my power and my voice
I stand tall and made my choice
To not let what you did define me, you can never win
I found my peace, I let the healing begin.

I thought you were on my side and was helping me move on
From the nightmares and hurt
But here we are again
A year later, the same day.
You knew how bad I felt about myself and took advantage of me
Was this the second part of the original plan
Taking what you wanted and leaving?
I thought I was healing bereft.
I trusted you once
But now I see the truth

You cared more about the plan to destroy me and yourself
And my heart was in the process of chaotic abuse.
But years later I am pulling through
To what I truly believed would come to you

Over ten years later, you got the wreck created
After all the pain, your karma was truly not G-rated.
I hope you learned a valuable lesson
To never pull someone down to bring up your adrenaline
I pushed myself hard to help those who I pray never end up like me
Blinded by a two-part plan, not being able to see.

In my blood run the colors of art
Passed down through generations, a painter's heart
From my great-grandmother's brush strokes bold and true
To my grandfather's masterpieces, each one anew.
My mother's hand guided mine with care
Teaching me the techniques, the secrets to share
Now it's my turn to carry on the legacy
A fourth-generation painter, proud and free.
With each stroke of the brush, I honor the past
Creating beauty that will forever last.
On every canvas, in every hue

I see the love and talent of those who came before me too.
I paint with passion, with skill and grace
Continuing the tradition, leaving my own trace.
A legacy of artistry, a heritage so grand
I am a fourth-generation painter, with a paintbrush in hand.

In the tangled web of fate, we find
A love that blossoms, pure and kind
Two souls that entwined, a bond so strong
But shadows lingered more on all the things that could go wrong.
I fell for you, my best friend's brother
A kindred spirit like no other
Autistic hearts that beat as one
A connection deeper than the brightness from the rays of the sun.
But in our love, a rift did grow
My best friend got pushed away, you know.
A casualty of our love's flame

A heartache that we tried but couldn't reclaim.
I never meant to cause such pain
To almost lose my best friend, it drives me insane
But in your eyes, I see the truth
A love that's pure, a love that brings back the feelings of youth.
So let's navigate this rocky road
Together, hand in hand, we'll go
For love knows no bounds, no limits, no end
My best friend's brother, hoping will be my forever friend.

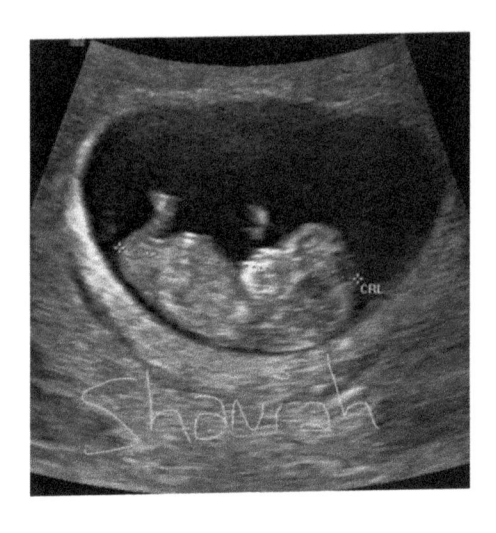

In the quiet of the night, I lay awake
Tears streaming down my face, one of the biggest heartaches
Four and a half months of joy, hopes, and dreams
Now shattered, torn apart at the seams
The pain is deep, the loss profound
A piece of my heart lost, never to be found
I struggled for years to accept, to understand
Why fate dealt me this cruel hand.
I felt lost, alone in my grief
Trying to find solace, seeking relief
But the emptiness inside remains
A constant reminder of my loss, my pains

I mourn for the child I can never hold
For the future that I wished for to never unfold
But in my heart, I know you'll always be
A part of me, for eternity.
I may never fully heal, and will never forget
But I'll cherish the memories, never regret
For you were a part of me, a pure love so true
And in my heart, I forever hold onto you.

In the darkness of despair, I stand alone
My heart shattered, my spirit overthrown
An hour before my grandmother's final breath
You chose to leave me, sealing my death.
I thought of you as my rock, my guiding light
But now I see you were never truly right
You abandoned me in my time of need
Leaving me to suffer and bleed.
As I sit by my grandmother's side
Watching her slowly slip away, my tears cannot hide
I think of all the memories we shared
And how you no longer cared.
I cursed the day you walked out the door

Leaving me broken and sore
But as I held my grandmother's hand
I know I must be strong-minded and stand

For she taught me to be brave and true
To face life's challenges, no matter what I go through
So I'll cherish her love and legacy
And let go of the agonizing pain you caused me.
Though you may have left me in the dark
I will find the strength to embark
On a journey, free from your chains
And honor my grandmother's memory, as she remains.
In my heart forevermore
A guiding light, a love so pure
And though you may have dumped me
I will rise above all the situations that will no longer continue to be.

Life is like a camera. Focus on what's
important and you will capture it perfectly.
—Josh Hutcherson

Once a family, now torn apart
By a decision that broke my heart.
A father walked away, leaving us behind
Leaving us homeless, with no peace of mind.
For nine long months, we wandered from couch to couch
Struggling to find shelter, something to eat, and money in our pouch.
My mom, my rock, tried to stay strong
But the pain and the fear felt so wrong.
I couldn't understand why he chose to leave
Why did he abandon us, causing us to grieve?
But through the darkness, a light did shine

With the love and support of friends and family so
 kind.
We may have lost our home and security
But we found strength in our unity.

Together, we faced the stormy weather
And emerged stronger, bonded forever.
Dad may have left us in despair
But we found solace in each other's care.
Though the wounds may never fully heal
We'll rise above, with hearts of steel.
So here we stand, survivors of the storm
Stronger, wiser, in each other's warm embrace.
We'll rebuild our lives, brick by brick
And show the world that we can still be thick.

In a sea of faces, unfamiliar and new
I walk the halls with a scar on my head
A reminder of the journey I've been through
A battle fought, a war that I've bled
Entering high school with trepidation
Feeling out of place, like a puzzle piece lost
I long for the comfort of my old situation
But here I am, facing this new cost.
The stares and whispers follow me around
As I navigate this foreign land
I try to blend in, to not make a sound

But the scar on my head, a mark so grand.
I feel like an outsider, a stranger in my own skin
But deep down, I know I am strong
I've faced the darkness, I've fought to win
I'll find my place, where I belong.

So I'll stand tall, with my head held high
Embracing my scars, my journey, my truth
I may feel out of place, but I'll give it a try
For I am a survivor, a warrior, a living proof.
High school may be tough, but I'll persevere
With courage and grace, I'll find my way
I'll show the world that I have no fear
And I'll shine bright, no matter what people say.

In the crowded mall, I saw his face
My old camp friend from fifteen years ago, a familiar embrace.
It had been almost nine years since we last spoke
But seeing him again, my heart awoke.
He asked me to be friends with benefits, just for fun
And foolishly, I agreed, thinking it would be a harmless one.
But as time went on, I fell for him once more
Only to realize he was just using me, nothing more.
He gave me a lot of mental issues, playing with my heart
Piece by piece, tearing me apart.
I thought our friendship could withstand anything
But now I see, it was all just a fling.

I should have known better, should have seen the obvious signs
But blinded by what I thought was love, I fell more in love with his lies
Now I'm left with scars that may never heal
A reminder of the pain he made me feel.
So as I walk away from him, my ex-friend of the past
I know that our friendship was never meant to last.
I'll pick up the pieces and move on from this mess
And learn to love myself more, and nothing less.

In a moment of pure delight
Receiving the news from my sister filled me with light
A precious baby boy soon to arrive
My heart swelling up with joy, I felt alive.
Declan Reece, a name so sweet
A new chapter of life to greet
I couldn't contain my happiness
Becoming an aunt, peaceful bliss!
Imagining the moments we'd share
The love and laughter we would both bear
I longed to hold you in my arms
To keep you safe from any disappointing harm.
Counting the days with glee

Anticipating the moments I'd see
Your tiny face, so pure and new
My heart overflows with love for you.

So precious, so perfect in my eyes, my little nephew
A bond so strong, forever true
I'll cherish every moment we spend
My sweet Declan Reece, my heart's new best friend.

To my sweet Kason Ryder, so dear
Your laughter brings me so much cheer
From the moment you came into this world
Playing "Stinky Feet," the giggles and amazing moments were truly earned.
Your tiny and chunky hands wrapped around my finger
A connection so strong, it made my heart linger.
In your eyes, I see a reflection of me
A bond that I hope lasts for eternity.

From singing Mickey Mouse Clubhouse to bedtime stories
Our moments together are filled with glories.
I cherish every hug and all the smiles
Knowing that with you, I'll walk many miles.
You bring so much joy into my life
With every giggle and every strife

I am grateful for the bond we share
For you, my dear Kason, I will always care.
You are my youngest nephew, my "Stink Bug" buddy,
Together we'll navigate life from being so muddy
I'll be there for you through thick and thin
For with you, my sweet Kason, my heart will always win.

Haily, I know I took up
So much of Mom and Dad's time
With all my sickness and struggles
I noticed it was hard for you to shine.
You've been there for me the best way you knew how
Even when you pushed me away
I know I haven't always shown it
But I continuously look up to you every day.
I see the sacrifices you made for yourself
The attention you've had to share
And I want you to know

That I appreciate how much you tried to care.
I know it's been tough for you
But please believe me when I say
That no matter what happened, I continue to love you

And I'm grateful for you every day.
So thank you, Hail, for all you do
It wasn't the easiest, but your love was true.
I may not always show it, but it's true
I love you more than you ever knew.

Your hands were never there,
To guide me through life's rough terrain.
It was always my mother's love and care
That shielded me from all the pain.
She was the one who held me tight
When I was scared and small
While you were either working
Or didn't want to be bothered at all.
You were always absent
Lost in your own world of vision and pride
Leaving my mother to be present

While she worked multiple jobs and on top of that,
    be my guide.
But despite your lack of care
I never felt alone or lost
For my mother was everything you weren't
No matter the emotional cost.

She was my rock, my guiding light
Through every story and every test
And though you were never right
My mother's love was always the best.
So thank you to my mom, who was both my mother
    and father, for all you've done
For being my strength and my guide
For being the one who's always won
The one who's always by my side.

To the strongest woman I know,
Mom, you are my rock, my guiding light
Through every dark and challenging night.
When seizures struck and left me scared
You were there, showing how much you cared.
In hospitals and therapy sessions
You were my constant, my greatest possession.
You never stopped, never gave up
Always there to fill my cup.
Your love and strength pulled me through.
I owe everything to you.

Thank you for being my pillar of support
For never letting me feel out of sorts.
Mom, you are my hero, my saving grace.
I am forever grateful for your embrace.
Thank you for all that you do
I wouldn't be half the person I am without you.
I can never thank you enough for your tireless support
For being my rock of every sort
You are my blessing, a guiding light
Thank you, my hero, my mom, for being my everything, day and night.

I rise from the ashes, more resilient than before
Through seizures and autism, I have endured
Lost friends and relationships left me feeling sore
But I am still standing, my spirit assured.
I am thankful for each breath I take
For the beating of my heart, for the sun's warm embrace
I am grateful for the challenges I've faced
For how they have shaped me, helped me find my grace.
I am alive today, against all odds
I have faced the darkness in my many, and emerged with a new resolve
I am thankful for the strength that lies within
For the courage to keep going, to never give in
So I stand here now, with gratitude in my soul

For all the obstacles I overcame, for every lesson learned
I am thankful for this life, for the chance to continue to grow
For being alive today, my spirit unburned.

About the Author

Lindsay Elle Waxman is a passionate twenty-nine-year-old writer with a love for the arts, Disney, and creativity. Writing has always been her escape, her way of exploring new worlds and diving into the depths of her imagination. Through the power of poetry, she shares the raw emotions, struggles, and triumphs of living with these conditions. Each poem is a glimpse into the inner workings of her mind, offering a unique perspective on the challenges and beauty of navigating health issues, friendships, and more.

From the fear and uncertainty of a seizure's sudden onset to the overwhelming sensory of everyday life with autism, Lindsay's poems capture the complexity of her experiences. Through the rhythm and flow of words, she hopes to convey the resilience and strength that have carried her through the darkest moments and the joy that comes from her unique neurodiversity.

This book is not just a collection of poems; it is a testament to the power of self-expression and the healing potential of art. It is a celebration of the human spirit's ability to overcome adversity and find beauty in the most unexpected places. Join Lindsay on this journey through the highs and lows of living her everyday life and discover the poetry that lies within the depths of her soul.

Printed in the USA
CPSIA information can be obtained
at www.ICGtesting.com
LVHW051619211124
797039LV00019B/445